The Rose Inside

THE ROSE INSIDE

POEMS BY DAVID KEPLINGER

NEW ODYSSEY PRESS
KIRKSVILLE, MISSOURI

First New Odyssey edition published 1999
Copyright © 1999 Thomas Jefferson University Press
All rights reserved
Printed in the United States of America

Author photo by Veronika Dyjakova

Cover illustration: Marc Chagall, *Hommage à Apollinaire/Homage to Apollinaire,* oil on canvas (1911-1912), reproduced by permission of Stedelijk van Abbemuseum, Eindhoven, The Netherlands.

Library of Congress Cataloging-in-Publication Data (Applied For)

Keplinger, David. , 1968–
    The rose inside: poems / by David Keplinger—1st New Odyssey ed.
    p.   cm.
    ISBN 0-943549-69-8 (alk. paper). — ISBN 0-943549-70-1 (pbk. : alk. paper)
    I. Title
1999

                                                                        CIP

New Odyssey Press is an imprint of Thomas Jefferson University Press at Truman State University in Kirksville, Missouri 63501 (*http://www2.truman.edu/tjup*).

The paper in this publication meets or exceeds the minimum requirements of the American National Standard—Permanence of Paper for Printed Library Materials, ANSI Z39.48 (1984).

For my mother and father

and for Minou

Contents

I

II

ACKNOWLEDGMENTS

Special thanks to my teacher Bruce Weigl, who provided guidance and support for many years.

Some of these poems first appeared as follows:

Southern Humanities Review ("Blessing for the Liver"); *Hayden's Ferry Review* ("Pawkatuck"); *Black Warrior Review* ("Mercy"); *Phoebe* ("The last sin...," "On the table...," "Eve, we should have..."); *Berkeley Poetry Review* ("The Last"); *The Chariton Review* ("House at the Graterford Prison"); *The Green Mountains Review* ("The East," as "Maple," "Oswiecim," as "Near Krakow"); *Northeast Corridor* ("Valley Forge").

I

BLESSING FOR THE LIVER

The heart with its lies
is a lesser thing, neither

dangerous nor kind,
the serpent, the lonely.

And the brain is where
the world once fell

from the smallest tree in the orchard,
the apple my great-grandfather

carves with a razor for eternity,
twirling it in his hands

to eat, the delectable
fruit we are too much of.

But cut the liver from my body intact,
which faced all my poisons.

No wonder it's the bearer
of the soul, stone at the end of my life.

THE EAST

1.
It's not a dream I've had,
the gleam of oil on my father's face,
the hanging bulb at night
shining from its metal cord in the garage,
things becoming electric in his hands,
in September when nightcrawlers
maneuvered through the wet
common grass of our properties:
it exists. In that light
I go to my own maple floating
something like stone, something
like idea, against the yellowed
field before the tractors.

2.
Affixed to the radio
to sharpen into jazz, samba, polka, big band,
was the tube that held sound,
the whole country
glowing in the frayed element
in September when I turned
eleven years old. The priest
asking for money came, the hallway
lit by a pearl revolver
I found in the velvet red box,
and the urge to kill. Bats clumped
high in the attic clutched their little
barrel chests. I knew the enemy
was in the room at night.
Behind my eyes his face bloomed.
And guns were going off
in all of our houses; Eisele
was thrown twenty feet

by a homemade bomb;
he told the paramedics the sun
hurt, he was all bloody
and the creek smoked
and gurgled, the chimney collapsed.

3.
It was the year of Maria's death.
The froth in her mouth not
milk, but like milk. We lived so
dutifully that year, and the man from the prison
who broke into the house
to drink a cup of water, he saw
how dutifully we had lain the table
how things could be fixed,
torn apart, rebuilt,
like my need to be forgiven, for what
I'll never know the right words.
We went on strike.
We worked, went on strike, became
journeymen, pipefitters, millwrights.
And Maria examined
her cancer like a scientist, her leg
breeching, obviously worse, while I watched
in my own science through the door.

4.
I might have spent the whole time running
from a God I can't trust,
God of the heaven above the slaughterhouse,
and one sewer in the east.
I was running from the millwright's sons
who were waving two-by-fours
crazily near the river.
I had a way to bleed.
I'd hold the pool of blood on my tongue

then spit. It was my one talent,
the kids hung around
though now I want peace
to the breaking down of things,
to the crayfish who came to life
in the quarry stone I lifted,
peace to the fluttering stomachs of field mice
eaten by maggots,
peace to the field, the nests of gypsy moths
knocked down from maples all summer,
their wormy young concealed in tiny sacs.

GRAVITY

He tells me he had wings.
This is how he calls attention
to the overgrown blades of my back

that rise when I work my shoulders. I've seen my father
climb the rusted pegs of a telephone pole
to change a fuse,

and wade to the edge of the roof with buckets of tar.
He's magnificent, his body in sunlight,
the day collapsing across our yard.

He eases one hand on my low
awkward shoulders, and the other on my chest
to push me straight.

PAWKATUCK

In father's recurring dream of his navy years,
he's guarding a clothesline on a tanker at sea.
It's midnight. The ship is called the Pawkatuck.

Pawkatuck: he says it in his sleep.
He shifts his weight one way, then the other, throws the rifle
to one side, then the other.

His face and mine contained in the one.
His nights pissing over the hull of the oiler's deck,
the long drunk of Spain, the broken

bottle on his head, the clothesline
from Chain Street with his boyhood
clothes out of place on a ship at sea.

Not even tomorrow will they reach a port of call.
And then he'll end up in Haiti,
or some other godforsaken place,
where children will lead him through the open markets
of oddly shaped fruits, and the funeral dance
that scares the devil away.

HOUSE AT THE GRATERFORD PRISON

1.
Saltweed in the garden, overhanging, banal.
She, in the house shucking
corn, at the sink overlooking the field.
The *hush* of wind, The people are sad, the child says
Those people are smoke, filtering out of cell windows at night
    Cornsilk falling away in water

2.
The child saw a dragonfly hovering
in the tall grass before the field.

If it was real, its wings were black-veined,
metal contraptions.

If he had words he'd say
it's all amiss, that he and this thing are

together in the world. From this point on he will feel
improbable; a thousand cracked mirrors

in the blacks and yellows will tell him so, the cruel
myopia of its inner eye.

3.
She guts catfish, heart,
liver, string of intestine, pieces

she can't identify, takes in her hand
the smell of sex,

the backbone
peeled away

head chopped, placed in a bag
then in another, whiskers

metallic, scaled, muddy smell of
the bottom, fried, peppered,

the boy doesn't like the taste
just catches them

to his great delight in the stagnant
pools below the Perkiomen bridge

Here is where he pried the hook
away from the eye, the half eye—

The belly's marked with black stars.
The taste is bad;

she will cook it in oil and lemon
and she will eat it.

4.
Fire came down to him.
In sleep it whispered
Destroy what I have made,
a blade of field grass,
rose, weed, and animate thing:
the blue speckled egg
whose embryo comes briefly to life,
huddled and tiny in the yolk,
and the serpent didn't escape him,
whose skin turns
to ash, nor its counterpart
the waterstrider, whom he scooped
from the surface of the pond
that afternoon where it glided in boring light,
and burned in the corn, the slow
crackling feelers curling under a match.

Inside: George Gaines at Graterford Prison, 1981

A point of moonlight
anchored through the barred window, and beyond that,
the field, the faraway, not-yet-created, wholly unearned world.

Night, a wall on four sides.
The smell of urine at the john. The shouting below.
From a piece of piping, he's sawed an edge to jab in the dark:

it has taken this long to find the means and the hours,
but always he comes back
to only himself, a cell, gravity pouring through his hands.

Small Critique of a Pencil Sketch

The line takes over. It fattens
the withered leg. It fattens the hip
her hand rests on. The line
would come as easily as sex: she'd lean back on the railing,
the ocean behind her, and I'd make my little sketches.

I have come to sit full days on the terrace alone,
with all the drawings I have of her.
To think of it now—
how slowly she undressed,
the crippled girl.

First her blouse,
her necklace, rings, finger by finger.
On the railing she'd lean back
and slide her dress
down both legs at once.

THE IMMACULATE
For Grace M.

I.

Before I could turn to face the loose horses
spooked, or act on his word
to move aside, father had lifted me
out of the tall grass, into the stable.

The smell of shit was like
a mouth on my lips. The seventy years
is only a minute. I stood there
while he calmed them with his voice.
Grace (he said to me), *You'll live long yet.*
Me, I'm filled with dirt.

We set the bridle into place.
The colt lowered her tongue on me—
here—and started to lick.

I don't think there's a word
for not being afraid, but knowing I should be.
It was dawn. The dark loaves
of bread were beginning
to swell in the pantry;
with a sponge he wet the flanks,
the tail, dusted with shit. Then he reached behind her
and washed the anus clean.

2.

Yes I felt—the instant you withdrew
from my opened gown—the baby come alive in the high bed.
You braced the headboard
with one hand, held me with the other
so the crucifix had fallen off the wall:
father,
I took that as a sign,

as now the face inside me
asserts its stern features,
like you are always inside me,
of whom I am afraid.
Who will believe
a life can come from nothing, a virgin no less?
No one fully grasps that sad story.
Your hands, black with pig slop,
mine fringed in light, our light...
I don't even know what I want from you.
I lower my face, simply
to please you.

The Method

The sea-pitch washed ashore
a claw. Its hinges white,
the pincers so smooth
that when I kicked it with my foot the thing
opened: you also came to life
in the hospice
three times until the medicine
faded in your dead brooding.
You closed your fingers in a fist,
like this.

An Omniscient Narrator Saying "Hold Still"

1. Leo Falco, 1901–1919
Leo's blurred face: on the yellow
photo plate his yellow hand
formless above the stock-still guitar,
counting each regular beat
coming down hard with the foot
as the one eye—implacable,
(even the eyelash is clear
and in focus) glances

2. Leonard Falco, 1900–1975
Two minutes on the road to Ohio
or back, the field of wildflowers
now grey behind them.
Leonard grips Leo too tight
to pose, as the father, unseen,
bends behind his standing camera,
and covers his face with the hood.

VALLEY FORGE

We wiped the sweat from our hands
to lift the coffin. Then nearly dropped him,
heavy now like stone.

Who can be ready when the horses come,
taking the fathers away? The markers, poised
like columns of salt, were nameless, line over line.

Here is what I saw: my father reached
to catch his father's body, far off
among the aster blossoms and opening stars.

II

ANOTHER CENTURY

The women who fan
their skirts before the stove,
they live in another century,

where, along the river
the columns of blackbirds
don't mind that we walk near them.

When the pig is cut from neck to belly,
the river freezes.
The slabs are cooked.

Smoke fills the kitchen. Nothing changes,
January comes with police and hard bread.
With January passes a hundred years.

On Vicolo San Lorenzo, I See My Family Name

A little waterfront not on the map.
The small blue boats with tires for life rafts
float along the dock,
where fishermen gather mornings.
A salamander skitters up an oar
and steals inside a tiny crack
between my eyelashes.
Four boats,
moored beneath the statue of Mary,
covered with lichens and gulls.
I want to think I'm someone else
but I'm always right here in my body,
my America. Here in my palm,
too small to be a fisherman's,
an aquamarine wave no higher than an inch
has come a long way
to rend itself.

FISH MARKET

Curse us if we cursed
the fish man hauling
blue tarps at market

some oceanic Friday
evening and the harbor
full wind, insignificant

as a handkerchief
and far, except for its smell,
which is—or is that

his hands? Love his hands.
The other skin
on his skin, memorizable,

like a good joke
and as vulgar,
its eyes, little wells of salt

that stare, even as he raises
his knife, at other times,
to cut them out.

The Last Days

We spent the last days fishing in the dam.
Simple living minnow, circling in a bucket,
I lifted you out with my hands.
Your tiny mouth parted. The hook slipped down your throat
and out the belly.

SAN CALOGERO HEALING SPRINGS
Sciacca, Sicily

Underneath a canopy
of ivy the Christ
with real iron
hammered in his hands and feet
hangs loosely on the bow
of his ivory spine,
where the grotto opens for visitors.
A nun in habit
sweeps the courtyard of a nearby spring
with a black straw broom
that fans out like palm leaves
and does little good.
A pile of lemons
gathered behind her
remains standing,
marvelously, in the sunlight.

FROM MY WINDOW, JANACKOVA STREET

Breath taste on the glass: winter.
(Crow survives it better than you.)
Behind that doorway there is fighting in tongues,
a lady and gentleman in house robes.
All morning her broken violets wilted on the sill.
She bends them dying into place.

RECONSTRUCTION OF AN ANCIENT THEME

1. *Territorial*
Then we came to the grave to light
the lamps, but found them lit by someone else
within the hour. Who before
her should light the beloved's red candles at her father's grave?
The dogs' yelps, as far as Krasna,
are a century behind me already,
or before me,
and the little jump in their vocal cords in evening, when they smell
     each other
is ready.
She blew the candles out, and lit them again.
I want her in the cabin's chill all night,
but again his face
presses into the dark.

2. *The Maps*
Nika traveled far to claim
the house her ancestors built in Krasna.
She called to the fathers, de-heavening them.
They live by star charts of their own.
She memorized her way
when the street signs were torn down
and the living quarreled with the maps—
whose maps were whose, who drew them first?
She flew above the ancient birches
twisted and white, as she slept.
I could hear her, moving her mouth in the old way.

3. *Puppet Theater*
That to move from one moment to the next ,
ungodly force and will are required, any puppet can tell me.
How did I, for example, arrive from our table at the castle garden in
     Krasna

to this winter room alone? Nika would say it
slowly, so I would understand, the simplest words
and the heaviest meanings—
we are carried. The puppeteer
walked his creatures to us, having them bow.
Nika kissed the forehead of the hunchback
(who covered up his face),
the one with zeroes for eyes.

KRASNA

I learned to trill the "r" in Krasna,
with Ferda whose face was withered,
sclerosis in his brain
like drowsy crow's wings.

The river ran its program: now.
The village was called Beauty.
"Say my name with the "r",
Ferda instructed,

in the tavern overlooking the synagogue
burned out and condemned.
However I say it,
it will never be clear.

The language of a place in time.
The river said, Get moving.
But Ferda told me,
Say my name.

Dramatic Pause

The creak of a chair
about to collapse
in a schoolroom built before the war.

The name on the door illegible.
The teacher of history to whom it belongs.
A stool for the outcast: the dunce or the prodigy.

REPRISE

In the flood were submerged
four henhouses, in the water
of the mad rivers.

Vladimir spoke only of
"the flood that destroys
and the flood that sustains."

The neighbors had named
his chickens after members
of the secret societies to which he'd belonged,

taking great pleasure
in the shrieking
at slaughtering time.

That a man's tragedy
is his impulse for narrative
within the lyrical fact of being in time

meant less and less
in a bare room of hanging crosses,
potatoes in a steel bowl, the storm.

Though it was high summer,
the green fields disintegrated
to a muddy brown.

Only the great mystery
that reveals itself
by other mysteries remained:

Vladimir tipping
the bottle over my cup, the click
of glass on glass.

The brandy pouring.
The henhouses empty
after the storm.

Many Forms of Yes

The old German quarter of Frenstat.
A long way from the forest
where the Jews were hidden.
Girl in a window undressing
slips a sweater over her head
which blindfolds her as you watch.
In the same window are the upside down
bouquets, the colors of stained glass.

OUTSIDER

She sang her work:
and worked her fingers through

my still-damp hair.
Across my throat,

and evenly over my face in the mirror,
she spread cream.

She soaked the blade
in water and raised it.

With her eyes she asked
if this was all right.

OSWIECIM*

Days the crowds emerge at three pm

in September performers emerge with their stands—

the doves unfold like paper
in a street magician's hands—

and the new money is good for bread
And the old money for salt, yeast, sugar

The old money in one pocket, the new in the other

On the table we keep a dictionary: it takes minutes for Nika to say
You are tender and me back: you are tender

The bath, the white tub, Turkish coffee on a white chair
For a long while

I've been too fast to talk, I should take my time

with words, the words are precious

An hour for the coffee on the fire

A dove

———

*Oswiecim is the Polish name for the city the German army called Aushwitz.

THE DOPPLER EFFECT

In the single,
creeping dogwood remembered
from myths his grandmother told,

and in the blossoms
themselves that cover this meadow
like soap flakes,

the sorry tulips with drooping heads
then last of all the words inside
the camp—these things fade

for the man who survived
his own life at the gates
of a city he can't believe now

he lived in. With him he could go
running through a field and wind up
thousands of miles away,

in Hungary, or all the way
to Tel Aviv, the kibbutz,
the ad firm in Manhattan,

so why can't I fathom him
come back to this rickety bridge I know
anyone could love,

watching children throw bread downriver,
so it glides back to them
as bottom dwellers surface?

There the dogs with muzzles
wander freely about, near cars
whose slick,

bluish whir of sound
bloats and fades
like an insect in the ear,

as he remembers words
for flowers while the flowers
somewhere feel their lives

called back: persimmons,
Mary's lace, dandelion, jonquil,
and rose.

What a sleep that was without a name,
a calamity! A calamity
where nothing can be dreamt or accomplished,

and those seconds without words occupy
whole days, or a year,
or a period of years.

From the bridge he sees fields
and wire fences, some cows,
a horse wagon filled with dung.

He is in love with the flight of seconds.
He sees the night train
passing at dusk as inside

a woman with yellow
fingernails eats a peach
in her two hands

and the Polish soldiers
with their tilted berets
sleep quietly on one another's shoulders.

Oswiecim, 1995

DISCRETION

Is the man next door.
A thin wall of a tenement
visited by hookers and drunks.

Midnight's click
of his bedlamp.
Me reading Miss Emily aloud in the bath,

the pages rustling
as I turn them. He
perhaps hearing

("—This is the Hour of Lead—")
while his people lazily turn in sleep.
He rises from his bed that creaks, gathering clothes.

The Distance between Zero and One

In April the carnival came.
The ice and the factory lot,
the carnival rides huffing black stripes of smoke....

Pig slaughter music.
My great love stirring the blood with her hands.
Others cleaning the long blue
intestines in snowdrifts
filled with tiny stones.

Rain Prospectus

*

At the end of Rorupvej stood the old house and cathedral.
The gardener smoking his pipe
walked on stones and dragged a hoe from the shed.
His son and I sleeping in down, in September
on the street of dwarf apples at the edge of the woods.

*

I was dreaming of the rafters of a train station
where I floated among doves who paced the eaves.

*

Of the things I remember:
a storm was coming, the windows sickly blue.
Later, the gardener's son climbed
the steeple with me following.
He heaved the black bell drum to call the thatchers home at noon,
the cold fields before rain.
The rope suddenly out of his hands into mine.
The panic of the wings.

Exactly

The night conductor
took his little

downward jump
at the Bohumir stop of my window,

the stop without one
cricket in refrain

the hanging light
in the station office

swinging as the conductor
tugged its metal chain

to switch it on
while over the table

he bent to eat
what was left for him there.

NEITHER HERE NOR THERE

To wake on the border train.
That one story you relive
(the hissing sound
you make love to)
for you is right here:
Tesin, two miles
and there is Poland.
The conductors call out
the moving cities;
they pass beneath awnings
where fruit is sold.
Someone saying *I*
louder than white sunlight,
the brilliant foamy
dust clouds above the mines.
When did the day get eaten,
revealing the next day?
You are neither this nor that
the woods say,
but when you sleep
you climb the same dogwood
in every nightmare
and every dream, branches
cut in unnatural angles, sometimes
on a blue background,
sometimes red.

BORDER

Beyond the border's balls of light
larger than even the moon,
and also before the border,
was another country.

You from neither
would remember men dressed as pallbearers
in a bar on that street,
who carried a slaughtered pig onto the dance floor.

The steam curling
the flesh where it was split,
delicious to the many dancers
spinning recklessly before the microphone's
nervous-looking singer.

Delicious as smoke in the beautiful mouths
of prostitutes who themselves
were indistinguishable
replicas of effeminate dignitaries.

There was a long wait, in the meantime,
to make it through the border,
where lights were too bright to see who waited,
likewise, on the other side.

EVENING CONVERSATION

I went days without reaching the next day.
I'd study the face of some pitiless Byzantine
who'd cringe and stare back,
cut into stone on the two-story rooftops.

When I close my eyes now
I still see those spires I travel with,
where the oldest women huddled at death notices
speak badly of the living.

On the ledge of the offices
the religious face of a crow, confirming it all.
The trains below exit: for Poland.
And as always, night coming.

A Clock Face without Hands

Nights I watch the insect
hover at the bed

cleaning its appendages
weightless huge wringing its hands

Lord you are in that way
above me too

beginning so dark and far
like the sound of dogs

shaking the chain-link fences
tapered in barbed wire

where crows perch carefully
in cliques and in the window

across the footpath
a red light goes out

The City beyond Existence

In that city, infinitesimal kites twirl and dive, the moon at midday
    rolling on its grooves.
Filled with the buses and lumber trucks which departing the stern
    seemed endless,
so like a magician's silk scarf pulled out of the sleeve, the ferry from
    Puttgarten took only an hour,
but how far from the city you left?, to those you left eating the
    twelve-pound carp for Christmas dinner,
which had lived for a week in the bath, all during the jokes of its
    death, how you would kill it,
open it up at the side still alive on the table, its head wrapped in wet
    cloth. The city beyond existence
is always the one you're approaching. Its moon, a ball bearing that
    slides on the ramp between midnights.

Where you come from for dinner you eat heart, blood-dark in the
    soup, you wait in line,
or observe the girl in the hall of the offices, who reminds you of her
who would sleep with a hand over her mouth, like someone afraid
    of what she knows.
So what was she doing there, always turning out of your vision
    towards the light of the marble windows?
You'd get up before dawn, the smell of your things filling a hotel
    room,
sex-stale (you two could turn it in a few hours into books and dried
    flowers laid on the table,
and wine spilled into the bed). Your sins were great but you found
    yourselves happy.

Dreams proved senseless by morning, all except the one in which
    you rent a bicycle in a foreign square,
and trying to ride it fall down. There are people standing around

who begin to laugh, which makes you sick,
or pretend to be hurt, so they bring you to a hotel room, where on
the walls are characters of a language
you can't understand. The bicycle lays in the bed along with you.
Next you are driving it into the fields of skunk cabbage,
while the crowds follow.

Did you think you were going back? Floating like that, but there
wasn't any place to go,
and if you grabbed for it it was like foil crumpling in your hands,
and then your hands crumpled.
Up there the air forbids itself. Your lover comes with her stickers
and prizes, you're a little boy with her.
You have lived almost everywhere, you sometimes think, and each
place has had its plans for you,
which deformed you. Then the freezer freezes shut and you go
hungry, a window comes off in your hands.
She hangs little flags around the room to remind you what you
should feel;
but you grow unimpressed. You want to open your hands and have
doves fly in, or the religions in their black rags.

Once, there was a month beside the tower, a tower wrapped in
circular ramps where horses drew telescopes
to the high observatory. You also went up. But you and the sky were
no closer.
On a pulley the smell of fish and salt from the harbor restaurants
would rise and fall all afternoon,
which brought you back down to the street. It was there you decided
that the smallest event required
infinite effort, and you were correct, remembering
the waterfall and the hundreds of pounds of force needed, once, to
make a swatch of wool.

Among the infinite cities, this is the one you left as a boy. The
        eclipse was coming. A star,
a nebula, deepened into form. You live there now like a ghost, incor-
        poreal, without voice or breath.
With the dancers at Tivoli whirling in time, spinning under white
        lights strung onto trees
and old-fashioned gas lamps surrounding the gardens. With the
        feeling in your mouth of other tongues,
the words for sleep and dream, the simplest abstractions.
Bare-chested boy in the window at dawn, when the harbor clouds
        break
you place both hands across your mouth—how unlike me, how far
        from me you are.

III

LINEAGE

I know what I know is uncommon.
Why do you think I'm so happy?

I make a shadow with my hands.
It makes no sense.

Did you ever see his shadow in the dark?
Did you ever see God's little shadow?

I press my hands together.
It makes no sense.

My ancestors are raping
the field for wheat again.
This time they've tied strips
of potato sacking over their mouths.
They've been at it a long time,
never stopping for a bite
of onion bread, stooped all day,
swishing their scythes at the ghost crops.
If I could get them talking
I would. But they know the old saying:
everything is heard by the Lord.
The gleaners bend quietly
like dogwoods, the makers of crosses.
Before they step on the wagon
they stop to make sure
the knots are good and tight.

The gypsy told me
Words, they're nothing,
It's better you had love.

She smiled when she spoke on these matters.

I was the child born
with his heart outside his body.
I watched it grow inside the womb.

I was the digger, stab of metal
splitting the earth.

I tied the ram, chanting a prayer at dawn
among my knives,

and I was a ribbon of smoke in the chimney,
an immolation, a blackening sky,

I was a field of locusts.

Eve, we should have started with you.
Me, I'm salt and blood,
but you would have helped that drunk
where he fell on the sidewalk,
his head cracked open.
I was the first man of the world,
drunk myself,
I didn't want to bloody my hands.
We should have started you from clay
instead of bone,
smooth so as not to splinter.

There was a garden;
it's overrun with names by now.
I could say the same for us:
where once the center
was the absence of center,
there's a place we call first love,
a voice among
the arrangements of shadows,
or over the telephone, the moon erased.
I want to get it right with words,
to name and possess it.
And here is the first mistake.

On the table, a statue of Mary,
surrounded by starlings,
a novena to Saint Jude
to be said for nine days.

It was me who put that rose inside your body.
Geese squawking a slow adagio,
dawn, the moon written out in chalk.

The last sin I committed
was naming the serpent.
I saw it in the tree
coiled in its shroud.
I tried to let the tongue's
split root speak for itself,
but don't you agree
the sound is hissing?
Don't you agree
snake is its body
as it lurches through the jonquils
in perfect theorems of thought,
vertebrae swishing
to twist around a stone, oh equal proportion
oh god of equations
oh fine way
the jaw unlatches to swallow an egg.

My bad eye crosses.
It makes my face more pitiable,
what was symmetry

the off-balanced gleam of the imbecile:
eye in its nothing pose,
drifting out of orbit.

The rest was easy:
the tumor tears in half,
begins again, and the work is good.

The molecule deviates.
The body vanishes.
The work is good.

ABOUT THE AUTHOR

David Keplinger was born in 1968. He has received grants and awards from the Open Society Fund, the Pennsylvania Council on the Arts, the Academy of American Poets, and the Katey Lehman Foundation. From 1995 to 1997 he was a Soros fellow in Frydek-Mistek, the Czech Republic, where he also sang part time with the jazz band "Dzezky Tesin." He lives in Philadelphia.

Cover design by Teresa Wheeler
Truman State University designer

The poems and text are set in ITC Legacy Serif 11/13,
a revival of Nicolas Jenson's excellent roman,
designed by Ronald Arnholm.

This book was printed and bound
by Thomson-Shore, Dexter, Michigan